HEY THERE, RALPHIE BOY!
THE LIFE AND TIMES
OF RALPH KRAMDEN

HEY THERE, RALPHIE BOY! THE LIFE AND TIMES OF RALPH KRAMDEN

Peter Crescenti

Rutledge Hill Press

Nashville, Tennessee

Photographs on pages 14, 16, 30, 51, 56, 58, 60, 70, 72, 91, 94, 110, and 114 courtesy of Personality Photos, Inc., and used by permission.

Published in Nashville, Tennessee, by Rutledge Hill Press, Inc., 513 Third Avenue South, Nashville, Tennessee 37210.

Typography by D&T/Bailey Typesetting, Inc., Nashville, Tennessee
Design by Harriet Bateman

Library of Congress Cataloging-in-Publication Data

Crescenti, Peter.
    Hey there, Ralphie boy! : the life and times of Ralph Kramden/Peter Crescenti.
      p. cm.
    ISBN 1-55853-178-5
    1. Honeymooners (Television program) 2. Kramden, Ralph (Fictitious character) 3. American wit and humor. I. Title.
PN1992.77.H623C64   1992
791.45′72 — dc20   92-15786
                                     CIP

Printed in the United States of America
1 2 3 4 5 6 7 — 97 96 95 94 93 92

To

Marvin Marx & Walter Stone
Leonard Stern & Syd Zelinka
Herb Finn & A. J. Russell

The men who put the skin on the bones
and the words in the mouths
of the funniest characters
in television history.

**A sincere "Thank You" to all those
who helped make this book possible:**

Larry Stone and Ron Pitkin, Rutledge Hill Press
Howard Berk, Viacom
Denise Marcil, Denise Marcil Literary Agency
MPI Home Video and CBS Video Library
Mike Nejad, photographer
"Daddy" and Howard Frank, Personality Photos Inc.

"Blessed is the man who trusts in the Lord,
whose confidence is in him."
Jeremiah 17:7

CONTENTS

INTRODUCTION

Is Ralph Kramden the "Big Wind" his wife, Alice, calls him, or the "Sweet Kid" Ed Norton is so fond of? The kindly bus driver who helps old ladies on and off the bus, or the grouch who is sent to the company psychiatrist by his boss? The big spender who throws hundred-dollar bills around like they were confetti, or the cheapskate who refuses to buy his wife a refrigerator?

He is all of the above, and more. A lot more.

There's so much to be said about Ralph Kramden — and there's so much Ralph Kramden to talk about. But Ralph is easily summarized in just one word: contradictions. He's a walking, talking, bus driving mess of 'em, so it's no wonder that it's hard to pin him down — even though he is a huge target.

Being the kind of guy he is it's no surprise that the people closest to Ralph find him hard to live with, yet impossible to live without. That's why Alice can be lowering the boom with a wisecrack about his weight one minute, and forgiving him for squandering the family savings the next. And why Ralph can throw Norton out of his apartment all the time and still count on his coming back the next day with a big smile and a "Hey there, Ralphie boy!"

The fact is, for all his shortcomings — too numerous to list here — Ralph is still lovable. More than that, his well-meaning but poorly plotted antics, his preposterous schemes, his overblown pride, and his Neanderthal way of thinking have helped elevate him to a preeminent position among TV characters. Just imagine how much poorer the world would be without the millions of laughs Ralph's big mouth and size-50 waist have inspired.

Laughter is what *Hey There, Ralphie Boy! The Life and Times of Ralph Kramden* is all about. It's Ralph in mouth-to-mouth combat with Alice and Norton, giving and taking — but mostly taking. When you think about it, has there ever been a better straight man than Ralph Kramden? If you're not sure, you will be by the time you've finished this book. Neither will you doubt that pound for pound, Ralph has generated more laughs than any man in history!

For those who prefer the braggadocio of Ralph Kramden, King of the Castle, to Ralph Kramden, the deflated blimp and penitent moax, there's lots here for you too as Ralph slings his own zingers at not only Alice and Norton, but at Norton's wife, Trixie, and Mrs. Gibson, Alice's mother.

Finally, no record of Ralph Kramden would be complete without an overstuffed sampling of his views on the subjects he knows best: marriage, manhood, women, money, and success.

Poor Ralph. If he had only measured himself by the number of laughs he's inspired, he'd have realized long ago that he indeed had hit that high note!

HEY THERE, RALPHIE BOY!
THE LIFE AND TIMES
OF RALPH KRAMDEN

I GOT A B-I-I-I-I-G MOUTH!

Alice: I'm not gonna help you make an idiot of yourself.
Ralph: I don't need your help, I'll do it myself.

Alice wants a "new" Ralph.

Ralph: All I know is, Alice was satisfied with me for fifteen years. Now she wants to change me.
Norton: She's got a nerve. She knew when she married you she was gettin' the worst of it.

Norton knows the score.

Ralph: Good thing I got a brain to figure things out for us.
Norton: You're right there, Ralph. You can really think of some smart things to get yourself outta the dumb things you get yourself into.

All's well that ends well, says Norton.

Ralph: Last night for dinner Trixie brought out two baked potatoes, one was a large one, one was a small one. Which one did you grab? The big one! That's the difference between you and me, Norton. If I grabbed first, I woulda grabbed the little one.
Norton: Well, what're you complainin' about, you got the little one!

Norton burns Ralph's bowling shirt while ironing it.

Ralph: Is this your idea of a joke, Norton?
Norton: No, no, that's my idea of a burn!

The Racoon Lodge costume ball is coming up, and Alice wants Ralph to make his own costume.

Alice: Why don't you use some originality? Show some ingenuity. Why don't you use your brain?
Ralph: 'Cause I wanna win first prize, that's why.

Ralph plans his summer vacation.

Ralph: I hope we get that same tent we had last year.
Alice: That oughta be easy. Tell 'em we want the one with the snake in it.

Ralph wants to hide his poker winnings from Alice.

Ralph: I could put it under the garbage can with a piece of tape. No, she'd see that when she emptied the garbage. There's a crack under that bureau...she'd see that when she was scrubbin' the floor. Outside the bedroom window there's a hole between two bricks. I could put it in there too. She'd find that though when she's bringin' in the laundry...
Norton: Why don't you give it to her, you don't have a chance!

Alice catches Ralph "in the act."

Ralph: I was practicin' playin' golf.
Alice: Oh, is that what it is? I thought it was football the way your backfield was in motion.

Norton thinks it's too much trouble to vote.

Ralph: You don't know what trouble is. Do you know what trouble some people went through to have you get the privilege to vote? In 1680 a small band of hardy pilgrims sailed for America on a boat called the Mayfair. It was a long, tough trip. They hardly had anything to eat. And when they landed in America it was a long winter. And on top of everything they had to fight Indians. Do you know why they did all this? Just so you could go to the polls and vote. Now what've you got to say to that?

Norton: Well, if they'd known I wasn't gonna vote, they could've save themselves the trip!

The guys have been playing cards, and Ralph's the big winner.

Brady: Goodnight Ed, so long "Lucky."
Ralph: You ever see a sore loser like that Brady?
Norton: Only once, Ralph. About three weeks ago, when you lost.

Ralph has bought a secondhand vacuum cleaner that doesn't work.

Norton: I think that motor needs a drop of oil.
Ralph: Yeah, that's what it needs, just a little drop of oil.
Alice: A drop of oil? It wouldn't help if you dipped it in Texas.

Ralph tries to make Norton feel guilty.

Ralph: How about that time we were playin' softball and you got hit in the head with a bat. Who got a cab and took you over to the hospital? I did. Who come up and saw ya every day? I did. Who brought you cigarettes and candy? I did.
Norton: Who hit me in the head with the bat? You did!

Norton bests Ralph at Ping-Pong.

Ralph: If he played fair I could beat him with both hands tied!
Norton: Yeah, if they were my hands that were tied!

Ralph's bragging again

Ralph: I'm the one in the family with it up here.
Norton: You got plenty of it down there too.

Norton plays Mr. Fix-it.

Norton: Don't you think it'd be a better idea if I went in there and plastered the cracks in the ceiling instead of you getting up on that ladder?
Ralph: So, you're tellin' me that I'm too fat and too heavy to climb this ladder, huh? Well why don't you say so?
Norton: I don't have to, you just did.

Ralph is working on a slogan for a contest.

Ralph: "Before I started eating delicious Slim-O Bread I weighed two hundred and fifty pounds. I now weigh…"
Norton: Two hundred and sixty pounds!

Ralph thinks Alice is having an affair.

Ralph: Everybody in the neighborhood probably knows it. I'm probably the laughingstock of the whole neighborhood. Tell me somethin' Norton, am I the laughingstock of the whole neighborhood?
Norton: Yeah, and they don't even know about this yet.

Ralph has been promoted to an office job at the bus company.

Ralph: Yessir, even when I'm president the bus drivers will be sayin' the same about me then as they say about me now.

Norton: Yeah, but when you get to be president you can fire 'em for what they say.

Ralph thinks Alice is pregnant.

Ralph: Here she is havin' a baby and I'm yellin' at her. Screaming and yellin' because I haven't got a hot supper. Boy, I'm nothin' but an ungrateful beast...I'm a no-good worm...I'm just a...uh...
Norton: Dirty bum!

Ralph thinks he's been hired to run an insurance company.

Norton: What's new, Ralphie boy?
Ralph: I'll tell ya what's new. Alice, how would you like to be the wife of a rich, brilliant, highly respected business man?
Norton: I think she'd rather stay with you, Ralph.

Norton has given Ralph spats for Christmas.

Ralph: I know it came from your heart.
Norton: No it didn't. It came from the Fat Man's Shop.

Honesty is Norton's policy.

Alice: This place looks like the Brooklyn version of Tobacco Road.
Ralph: That's your version of it. Norton, don't you like the furniture around here?
Norton: Ah, yeah, I like it all right.
Ralph: There y'are, Norton likes the furniture around here.
Norton: Of course, I don't live here.

Ralph and Norton have bought a broken-down hotel.

Ralph: When the girls get here don't make any cracks. This is the first time they're seein' the place and I want them to get a good impression. So keep your mouth shut.

Norton: If you want 'em to get a good impression, keep the door shut.

I GOT A B-I-I-I-I-G MOUTH!

Ralph thinks Alice has left him.

Ralph: Everything in here reminds me of her. The potatoes she peels, the Fridgidaire she fixes, the floor she scrubs, the dishes she washes. Norton, why did she leave me?

Norton: You just gave four good reasons.

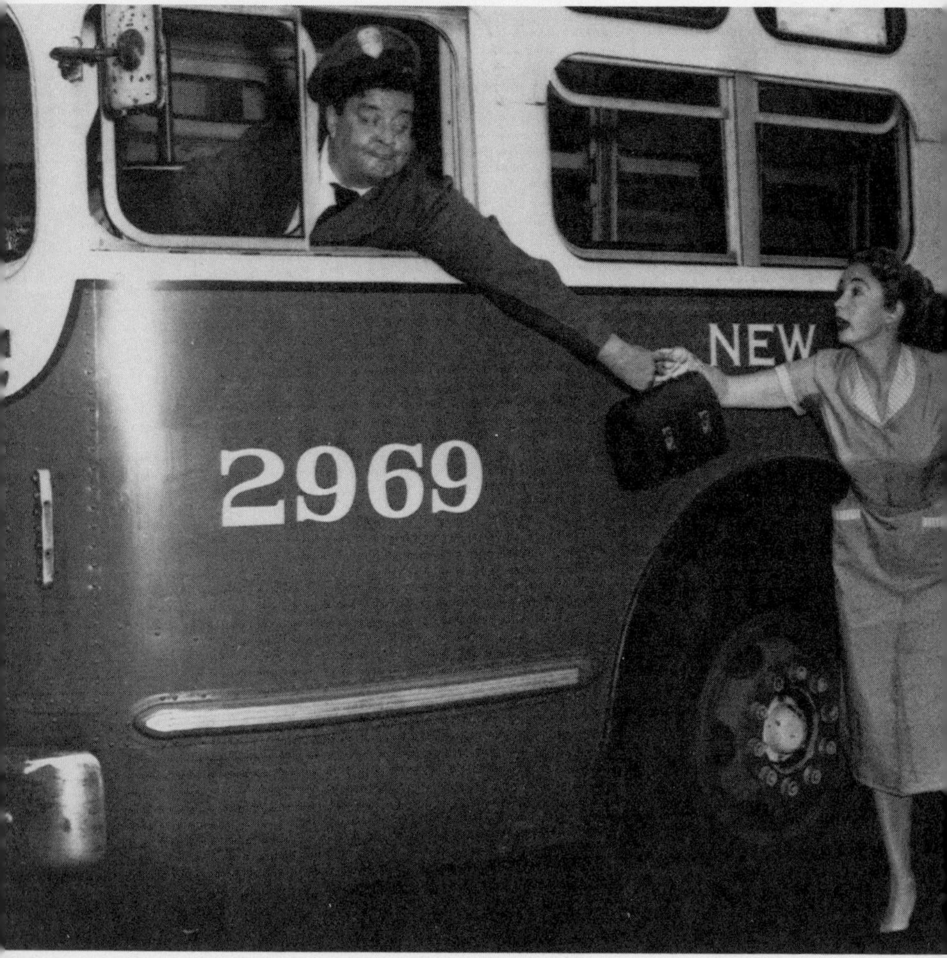
NEW
2969

ALL THE WORLD LOVES A FAT MAN

Norton: I'm tellin' you, Alice, you can be pretty proud of that husband of yours. All he thinks about is buses. He eats, drinks and sleeps buses. He's even built like one.

34   ALL THE WORLD LOVES A FAT MAN

Norton calls it like he sees it.

Ralph: Take a look at me. Go ahead, look me all over. Now describe my build.
Norton: Well, I'd say you have very well-developed muscles, got good bone structure, very good bone structure, fine frame...and the whole thing is covered with fat!

Norton needs a table cloth.

Alice: What have I got in the house that's large enough to cover that big table of yours?
Norton: How about a pair of Ralph's white shorts?

Alice wants to move in with her folks when Ralph loses his job.

Ralph: I am not goin' to your mother's. The apartment is too small for us.
Alice: Too small? You didn't think that when we lived there for four years. And that apartment hasn't gotten any smaller.
Norton: No, but Ralph's gotten bigger.

Ralph wants a vote of confidence.

Ralph: I don't care if you got any confidence, because I got enough confidence in me for the *both* of us.

Alice: You've got enough *everything* in you for the both of us!

Alice and Trixie have left their husbands and Ralph's the new cook.

Norton: What's for dinner?
Ralph: Frankfurters and beans.
Norton: Franks and beans?
Ralph: Yes, franks and beans. Whattsa matter with it?
Norton: Look, we been separated from the girls about a week now and we haven't had a decent meal since. I'm losin' my strength, I gotta have a decent meal. This afternoon in the sewer I was so weak I had to wear an inner tube to keep from drownin'!
Ralph: Will ya stop beefin'. I'd like a decent meal too. This stuff is wearin' me down.
Norton: Yeah, I can see you're wastin' away to a blimp.

Ralph thinks he's going to be a father.

Ralph: I got the name for the kid. I'll name him after me, Ralph.
Norton: That's a little confusing, isn't it, two Ralphs in the same family?
Ralph: Not necessarily so. I was named after my father. They used to call us Big Ralph and Little Ralph.
Norton: Who was your father, Little Ralph?

Ralph has learned his lesson.

Ralph: I'm gonna learn from here on in how to swallow my pride.
Norton: Well that ought not to be too hard, you've learned how to swallow everything else.

Ralph has run into Bill Davis, an old school chum.

Bill Davis: I was just thinking of the thing I wrote in your autograph book.
Ralph: What thing in my autograph book?
Bill Davis: "Some kids are small, some kids are tall, fatso Kramden is the only kid that walks down the hall wall to wall."

Norton gets pushy.

Ralph: Just remember, you can push me so far and no farther.
Norton: I can't push you at all. That's a job for a bulldozer.

Ralph thinks he's going crazy.

Norton: You could have a split personality, you know, like you're two people.
Ralph: Never mind, Norton, never mind.
Norton: You're big enough to be three people.

How can anyone so round be so square?

Ralph has bragged that he once saved Jackie Gleason's life.

Norton: How'd you save his life?
Ralph: I was drivin' down Madison Avenue and he was crossin' the street and I stopped for a red light. Well, if I'd've gone through the red light I mighta hit 'im! I saved his life, didn't I?
Norton: Look, by not hittin' Jackie Gleason you didn't save his life, you saved your bus!

Ralph's a contestant on a quiz show.

Ralph: Yessir, this is the time I'm gonna get my pot of gold.
Alice: Just go for the gold, you've already got the pot.

Ralph has bragged that he's boss in his house.

Bus driver: I really mean it, you're twice the man I am, Ralph.
Norton: Yeah, with about twenty pounds left over.

The feisty maid Ralph has hired is giving him and Norton a hard time.

Ralph: This happens to be my guest and I am your employer!
Thelma the maid: Some guest and some employer. The simp and the blimp!

Norton gives Ralph a new nickname.

Norton: Alice used to call you her Little Buttercup?

Ralph: Yeah. What's so funny about that, Norton?

Norton: You were a little cup o' butter, now you're a whole tub o' lard!

Ralph needs a ride.

Ralph: Are the guys pickin' you up in a car to take you to work?
Norton: Yep.
Ralph: Can you give me a lift?
Norton: Sure, always room for two more.

Ralph and Norton can't agree on what to watch on their TV.

Norton: If I go that set goes with me.
Ralph: That set goes over my dead body.
Norton: I couldn't get it out over your dead body. Whaddya think I am, a mountain climber?!?

Ralph and Norton are feuding.

Ralph: You are the only man that can turn my stomach upside down.
Norton: There ain't a man in New York City that's strong enough to turn your stomach upside down!

Ralph explains how he's won a safe-driving award.

Ralph: A group of men are picked to do a job, trained in the same fashion as each other, and there's always one man in the group that stands out far in front of the others.

Norton: If you stood out any more in front you wouldn't be able to get behind the wheel of a bus.

Norton thinks Ralph has died.

Norton: He must be approaching the Pearly Gates right now. At this time they're probably tearin' down part of the fence to let him in.

The Kramdens have adopted a baby.

Ralph: If he starts to cry I'll walk 'im up and down the floor all night.

Alice: Oh no, Ralph, if he wakes up during the night I'll walk the floor with him.

Ralph: Now don't start anything Alice, I'll walk the floor with him!

Alice: You need your sleep, Ralph. I'll walk the floor with him.

Norton: Let Alice do it. When Ralph walks the floor, nobody sleeps.

Ralph's bragging has caught up with him again.

Alice: What's the idea of telling that kid all those wild stories about yourself?

Ralph: It was your idea to get friendly with 'im, wasn't it?

Alice: Yeah? Well I didn't tell you to tell him all those fantastic stories. Golden Gloves champion, football star, Eagle Scout. And there's one thing I'd like to know, Ralph. When was the last time you lifted four hundred pounds?

Norton: This morning when he got outta bed.

Gee, I never knew Davy Crockett was so fat.

Ralph has made a stirring speech about manhood at the Racoon Lodge.

Norton: Ralph, I gotta hand it to you. You're a rotten Ping-Pong player but you make a good speech maker. If you were ninety pounds lighter the boys would have carried you out on their shoulders.

Ralph thinks he's dying of a rare disease and he's concerned about Alice.

Ralph: I'm goin' in six months and I've got nothin' to leave her, not a cent.
Norton: Look, as long as you're goin' anyway, why don't ya sell your body to science. If they pay by the pound she'll be left a millionaire!

Norton gives a lesson in slang.

Ralph: What does "icky" mean?
Norton: I don't know, why?
Ralph: Alice just said I was icky.
Norton: Must mean fat.

Norton is teaching Ralph how to dance the Hucklebuck.

Norton: You're supposed to waddle like a duck.
Ralph: How can I waddle like a duck?
Norton: It's easy...just walk like you always do.

Norton describes his mother-in-law to Ralph.

Norton: And is she fat! From the front she looks like you from the back.

Ralph wants to buy a candy store.

Ralph: When we take over we'll modernize the whole joint. We'll get a griddle in here, we'll start sellin' hamburgers, hot dogs, flapjacks, pizza pies.
Norton: Then we'll widen the front door.
Ralph: Why will we widen the front door?
Norton: Well, with griddle cakes, hamburgers, and hot dogs in here, how're you gonna get in and out the front door?

Ralph and Norton are feuding…again.

Ralph: From here on in we are deadly enemies. If you see me comin' down the street, get on the other side!
Norton: When you come down the street there *ain't* no other side!

Trixie and Ralph are fighting about one of Ralph's failed schemes.

Trixie: Maybe you can talk to Alice like that but you're not gonna push me around!

Ralph: Boy, if you were only my size!

Trixie: If I was I'd be the Fat Lady in the circus!

Ralph has been bragging to a kid in the building.

Tommy: Did you know Mr. Kramden when he was a football star? He was an end, a great end.
Norton: Great? Probably the *biggest* end in the business!

Ralph has trouble at the bus company.

Ralph: Who has to climb on my bus this afternoon? A company inspector. And what do you think that chowderhead had the gall to say to me? He says, "Kramden, this is a warning, you are getting too fat to drive a bus." He says, "If you get much fatter you won't be able to get behind the wheel." I was so steamed I wanted to get up and throw him off the bus!

Norton: I don't blame ya, Ralph, why didn't ya?

Ralph: I couldn't squeeze out from behind the wheel.

A Broadway producer is flattering Ralph to ensure his support for a play at the Racoon Lodge.

Producer: Mr. Norton, did you notice when he came in how his voice filled this room?
Norton: I did notice that the room got a little crowded. I didn't realize it was his voice.

TO DREAM, PERCHANCE TO SCHEME

Ralph: Nobody's one hundred percent, Alice.
Alice: You are. You've been wrong every time.

Alice is sick of Ralph's schemes.

Alice: Every week you come home with some new crazy hare-brained scheme. That's all I've heard for the past fourteen years, one crazy hare-brained scheme after another. That is all I have heard since the day we got married.

Ralph: You heard one of my hare-brained schemes before we got married...I proposed to ya!

Alice refuses to give Ralph money.

Alice: We are saving that money for an emergency.

Ralph: We've been married for fourteen years and for fourteen years you've been givin' me that same line. When I wanted to buy that television set you said, "Don't touch the money, suppose one of us gets sick." I wanted to buy the car, you said, "Don't spend the money, suppose one of us gets sick." You know what's gonna happen? All our lives we'll probably save a thousand, maybe two thousand dollars, and d'ya know what's gonna happen? Neither one of us'll get sick and we'll be stuck with the money!

This is the household utensil of the future. This's got everything, it does everything. It opens up cans, it takes corks out of bottles, it cores apples, it scales fish, it's got a screwdriver attachment, it cuts glass, it sharpens scissors, and there's a little thing here to take corns off your feet.

Ralph wants Norton to invest in a hair restorer.

Norton: You gave me the chance to be a millionaire with that shoe-shine stuff that glows in the dark.

Ralph: That was shoe polish. Look, do you know how many people there are with bald heads?

Norton: All I know is, there's twice as many shoes as there is bald heads and we lost money on that.

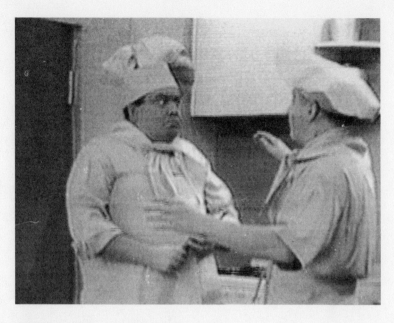

Ralph needs a partner.

Ralph: I am gonna make a fortune and I am gonna let you in on the deal.

Norton: Here we go again!

Ralph: What kind of a crack is that?

Norton: I'll tell you what kind of a crack that was. You've come to me before with a chance to make a fortune. I can't stand to make a fortune again...I'm goin' broke!

Alice won't give Ralph money for his latest scheme and he doesn't have anything to pawn to raise the money.

Ralph: That's exactly why I wanna buy the hot dog stand. Just so I can make some money so I can buy somethin' so I'll have somethin' to hock when I need it.

Alice rains on Ralph's parade.

Alice: Listen, Ralph, what d'you know about running a hot dog stand?

Ralph: Whaddya have to be, an Einstein to open up a hot dog stand? All you have to do is wait for Sunday, the roads are jam packed with cars. You buy a thousand hot dog rolls, a thousand hot dogs and you sell 'em. What can happen?

Alice: It can rain on Sunday.

Ralph: Every time I try to better myself you gotta put a block in front of me. The time I wanted to go into the used tire business you said nobody'd buy used tires. Then I wanted to go into the rug shampooin' business,

(Continued)

you said nobody wanted to have their rugs cleaned. Now that I hit on a perfect scheme, a hot dog stand, what d'ya do? You gotta make it rain on my busiest day!

Norton recalls a bum deal.

Ralph: It can't lose.
Norton: It can't lose, huh? That's what you said when we bought that parking lot next to the space where they were buildin' the movie house. You said, "People are goin' to the movies, they gotta have a place to park their car."
Ralph: How did I know they were buildin' a drive-in theater?

Ralph and Norton become CEO's.

Ralph: Soon this will be our business.
Norton: We will be respected business members of the community. We'll get invited to join country clubs, Alice and Trixie'll have fur coats. I'm tellin' you, this is gonna make us rich, this is the dream of a lifetime.
Ralph: Yep, our own hot dog stand!

Ralph and Norton are partners in a hot dog stand.

Ralph: Sunday will be our big day. About a thousand cars have gotta pass the hot dog stand. Out of every hundred cars, at least ten are gonna stop at our place. That's a hundred cars. Now in each car there's at least four people. Now if they each want hot dogs and soda pop that means that we'll have to serve four hundred hot dogs and four hundred bottles of soda pop every hour for twelve hours on Sunday.

Norton: I'd like to ask you a question. Could I have Sundays off?

*Ralph buys a piano because he wants to be a
songwriter.*

Alice: Now get this straight, that piano is not staying
here, you're taking it back.
Ralph: Now I know the reason. Now I know the reason
for Schubert's Unfinished Symphony...his wife made
him take the piano back!

Norton reminds Ralph of his failures.

Ralph: You're gonna miss your big chance just because a couple of my ideas went a little sour before?
Norton: A *little* sour?!? Boy, that's the biggest understatement made since General Custer said, "Over that hill I think they're friendly Indians."

Ralph tests Norton's marketing knowledge.

Ralph: Suppose somebody's got something and they want to sell it. How do they do it?
Norton: Well, the first thing they usually do is look you up and then sell it to you.

IT'S A MAN'S MAN'S MAN'S MAN'S WORLD

I'm the king. The king of my castle! I'm just like Richard the Lion-Hearted. I rule with an iron hand!

74   IT'S A MAN'S MAN'S MAN'S MAN'S WORLD

Alice needs help.

Alice: We are getting a maid.
Ralph: Whaddya mean we're gettin' a maid? I can't even afford you!

Ralph has won big at poker.

Ralph: This is the first time I've had any money of my own. You don't know what I have to go through when I wanna get something. Couple of months ago I wanted to get a bowling ball. You never saw such a riot take place. Arguin', screamin', yellin', rantin' and ravin'. I finally had to say to her "I'm the master of this house, give me the money for the bowlin' ball!" Then about three weeks ago I wanted to get a fishin' rod, the same thing all over again. A couple of days ago I wanted to get a wallet, she started in. I had to put my foot down again. I said "Gimme the money!" This time I'm keepin' the money and I'm gonna get what I want without any beefin'.
Norton: Whaddya gonna get with it?
Ralph: Gonna get a bowlin' ball, a fishin' rod, and a wallet.

*I should've known what I was in for, Ralph,
when you took a bowling ball along on our
honeymoon.*

Ralph: I am the boss of my household. I'm the one that gives the orders. I'm the one that makes all the decisions. On the day we were married I said two things: One, "I do," two, "I'm the boss."

Ralph advises a friend on husband-wife relations.

Ralph: Tomorrow afternoon when Agnes says "I do," that is the last decision you allow her to make. From there on in, show her who wears the pants.

Ralph thinks Alice is going to have a baby.

Ralph: Last week I was yellin' at her 'cause she didn't sew a button on my shirt. The week before that I was yellin' because she didn't press my pants and sew a seam on my windbreaker. But I'm tellin' you somethin', now that the baby's here everything's gonna change.

Norton: Whaddya think the baby's gonna be, a tailor?

Alice has been taking dancing lessons.

Ralph: Your mambo days are over. You wanna wiggle, wiggle over to the stove and get my supper.

Ralph doesn't want to bring Alice on a fishing trip.

Ralph: I catch the fish, you cook the fish. The only time we're together is when we eat the fish.

Ralph thinks he's been fired and Alice wants to get a job.

Ralph: I told you once, I told you a thousand times, when I married ya you were never going to work again in your life.
Alice: Honey, it won't be for long.
Ralph: I don't care how long it is, Alice, I got my pride. Before I see you go to work I'd rather see you starve.

Ralph has overheard Alice rehearsing her part in a play and thinks she hates him.

Ralph: The one thing that got me was when she said whenever I kissed her she got violently sick.
Norton: How do you feel when she kisses you?
Ralph: I get weak, knees tremble, I break out in a sweat...
Norton: How do you like that? She makes you sick too.

I treat you like a woman, I let you sew, I let you cook, I let you wash the windows, I let you clean up. Boys don't do that, Alice.

A new neighbor, Carlos Sanchez, has helped Alice carry her laundry basket.

Carlos Sanchez: You know, Mrs. Kramden, you shouldn't be carrying heavy things like this, not with those delicate hands of yours.

Alice: I wish somebody else around here would be concerned about things like that.

Ralph: Wait a minute. Wait a minute! If I told you once I told you a thousand times not to carry a heavy wash like that. Now the next time you have a heavy wash like that, make two trips!

Alice feels neglected.

Alice: You seem to have forgotten that *I* am a woman.
Ralph: *I* forgot that *you're* a woman? How could I,
you're always yappin'!

I know why you married me, Alice. Do you know why you married me? Because you were in love with my uniform.

Ralph advises Norton on being the man of the house.

Ralph: A man's home is his castle, and in that home he's a king. "I'm king of the castle and you're nothin'!"

Norton: Ralph, them words should be recorded and played at every wedding instead of "Here Comes the Bride."

Alice is making dinner.

Ralph: What's that?

Alice: Tuna fish. We're gonna have tuna fish salad.

Ralph: Tuna fish? What am I, a cat or something?

The Kramdens have adopted a baby girl.

Norton: Maybe she's hungry.

Ralph: Maybe you're right. Look in the icebox, see if there's anything to eat.

Norton: Ralph, there's some hamburger in here.

Ralph: Are you outta your mind or somethin', givin' my kid hamburger. She'll have steak or nothin'.

Ralph lays down the law.

Ralph: Let's not do any hollerin', screamin', or yellin'. You are not going on the fishing trip.
Alice: I am going.
Ralph: You're not going!
Alice: I am going!
Ralph: You're *not* going!
Alice: I *am* going!
Ralph: The only place you're goin' is to the moon!!!

Kramden Lecture #405.

Ralph: If you love me you're supposed to stick up for me. All other wives stick up for their husbands, even when they're wrong. And I'm right all the time. I'd stick up for you! Whether you were wrong or right. And you're wrong all the time!

Ralph thinks Alice is having a baby.

Ralph: I'm gonna be a father! I gonna name him Ralph, Ralph, Jr., after me. Maybe I'll name 'im Ed, Jr., after my father. Maybe Mike, Jr., after Alice's father.
Norton: Wait a minute, suppose it's a girl?
Ralph: Are you crazy? My son, a girl?

Alice wants Ralph to take her out on New Year's Eve.

Ralph: Why should I spend a whole week's salary on one night? For what? To go to a smoky nightclub, see a lot of chorus girls come dancin' out, people comin' over to your table drinkin' liquor, then at twelve o'clock they all go nuts...they yell "Happy New Year" and start kissin' people they never even met before.
Norton: Hey, too bad we can't go without our wives.

Alice wants a night out.

Alice: I got news for you, we're goin' out because once in a blue moon you take me out!
Ralph: Well, tonight the moon is yellow so get my supper ready!

Ralph and Alice in the Battle of the Sexes.

Alice: You men just think that you own this world.
Ralph: Yeah, but you women get revenge…you marry us.

Ralph is out of work.

Ralph: We'll just have to cut out a few luxuries.
Alice: All right, how about you giving up bowling?
Ralph: Now let's not get panicky.

Alice thinks Ralph's too gullible.

Alice: You are the original sucker. Absolutely anybody can pull the wool down right over your eyes. All anybody has to do is give you a smooth sales talk and you'll fall for anything.
Ralph: Maybe you're right. I married you, didn't I?

I SAID IT MY WAY

The guy's enough to drive you nuts. He hasn't got any consideration for anybody. I'm tellin' you, if he wasn't my best friend I wouldn't have nothing to do with 'im.

94

Ralph's fretting because he thinks he's lost his job.

Ralph: I only went to the sixth grade. I shoulda went through high school and then college. Huh, that wouldn'ta done any good anyway. That would even've made things worse.
Alice: What do you mean?
Ralph: How do you think I woulda felt, a college graduate gettin' fired by a bus company?

Alice's sister has gotten married.

Alice: What a beautiful bride Agnes made.
Ralph: Why shouldn't she? She's been practicing for twenty years.

A doctor has suggested that Norton's sleepwalking problem is caused by nerves.

Ralph: Sleepwalking isn't caused by nervousness.
Alice: Well how would you know?
Ralph: How would I know? I happen to be a bus driver, and if nervousness caused sleepwalking I'd be goin' through Australia right now.

When I'm in the right, I'm in the right. Nobody pushes me around.

Ralph thinks Norton's jealous.

Norton: Me jealous of you? Listen, Ralph, I can do anything better than you can. *Anything* better than you can. How come in the street when we play stickball they always choose me first? I'll go you one better, they never even start the game until I get there. How do you explain that?
Ralph: Because you're the only one who can get the ball when it goes down the sewer, that's why!

Ralph's making a sandwich.

Norton: What kind of peanut butter is that, is that the crunchy kind?
Ralph: Yes, it's the crunchy kind, and I can prove it to ya. When this jar hits your head, you'll hear a crunch!

A typical Racoon Lodge meeting.

Norton: I have the floor. You're out of order.
Ralph: The only thing out of order here is your head.

Ralph advises Norton on how to get a promotion.

Norton: Suppose they don't wanna give me the promotion?

Ralph: Then you scare them to death. Tell 'em you quit. Tell 'em after seventeen years in the sewer you're finally washing your hands of the whole thing!

Ralph's broken up with Norton and his new "best friend" washes cars for a living.

Alice: Well, they got one thing in common, they both work with water.

Ralph: Yeah, but Teddy uses it before it gets to Norton.

The Racoons want a celebrity to host their annual dance.

Norton: Hey, I had an uncle who went to school with one of the Marx Brothers.

Racoon president: One of the Marx Brothers? Say, that's wonderful. Which one?

Norton: Zeppo.

Ralph: Will you sit down. And if the Marx Brothers ever need another brother you can qualify as Nutso.

It's my nature to spend...except I never have anything to spend.

Madison Avenue takes its toll.

Ralph: You couldn't get me out of this house tonight if you told me that Jane Russell was runnin' a party upstairs and she couldn't get started till I arrived.

Norton has banged his head while sleepwalking.

Norton: Whatcha call the doctor for, all I got is a little bump on the head.
Ralph: I didn't call the doctor on account of the bump *on* your head, I called the doctor on account of the bump *in* your head.

Norton wants to borrow a handkerchief.

Norton: How about this one?
Ralph: That's one of my new ones. Remember, just wear it in the pocket. It's for showin', not blowin'.

Ralph and Norton have met the neighborhood teenagers.

Norton: Those kids remind me of me when I was a youth. I acted silly like those kids. But I guess as time goes on I grew older, I matured.
Ralph: Yeah, now you're a full-grown nut.

Ralph's having trouble with an aptitude test.

Norton: You can't push a square block into a round hole.

Ralph: No? Then how did you get your head in your hat?

*Fifteen years driving a bus. In all kinds of
weather. Through the rain, the snow, and the
sleet. You know that sign they have in the post
office, "The mail gets through no matter what
kind of weather." Do you know why? Because
the mailman rides with me!*

Norton has taken up astrology.

Norton: You were born under the sign of Taurus the bull, I was born under the sign of Pisces the fish.
Ralph: You were born under the sign of Pistacchio the nut!

I go down to the depot and get into my bus, and then for eight hours it's just me against Madison Avenue!

RALPH'S GREATEST SPEECHES

RALPH'S GREATEST SPEECHES

Ralph is mad because Alice won't give him the money to invest in a hair restorer.

Ralph: This doesn't surprise me. This doesn't surprise me. I knew what you were gonna say. I can read you like a book. On my way home tonight I said to myself, "No matter how good the proposition is, she'll be against it." Well, probably it's just as well. We wouldn't know what to do with a million dollars. We wouldn't know what to do with it. You'd be uncomfortable in a Cadillac. You'd get lost in a mansion. You wouldn't know how to put on a fancy dinner for people in gowns and tuxedoes. No, no sense in tryin' to improve ourselves, we might as well stay just as we are...poor, low, miserable human beings!

A reporter has stopped Ralph and Norton on the street and has asked Norton who is the boss in his house. After declaring that he's the boss, Norton asks the reporter not to print his remarks because he's afraid Trixie will see them. That's Ralph's cue to step forward.

Ralph: Well, Norton, you've just proved something to me that I suspected about you for a long time.

Norton: What?

Ralph: You're afraid of Trixie.

Norton: Hey, wait a minute, you're in no position to talk to me like that. No, no.

Ralph: You're not infering…? All I know pal is that if he had asked me that question I woulda said without hesitation that I am the boss in my household. I'm the one that gives the orders. I'm the one that makes all the decisions. Huh, on the day we were married I said two things: one, "I do," two, "I'm the boss."

Reporter: Pardon me sir, what is your name?

Ralph: Ralph Kramden.

Reporter: Ralph Kramden. Mr. Kramden, I'm gonna print what you just said, okay?

Norton: Go ahead, go ahead, go, go, answer him, big shot. Go on, go on!

Ralph: Heh, go ahead and print it.

Norton: He's a bus driver and he lives in Brooklyn.

Reporter: Thank you very much Mr. Kramden, you'll be in tonight's paper. Goodbye men.

Norton: Ho ho hee hee!

Ralph: What're you laughin' at?

Norton: I was just picturin' what you're gonna look like in a French Foreign Legion uniform!

Ralph: Are you tryin' to tell me that I'm afraid of Alice?

Norton: We're buddies for a good long time Ralph, I

know you pretty good. Now just take a little advice, get on the phone and call that newspaper and tell them to hold the presses, stop the presses and don't print that statement.

Ralph: Oh no, not me Norton. That's the kind of a thing that you'd do, but not me. And that's the difference between us Norton, that's the difference. I am a boss, you are a mouse.

Norton: Well, I got one more thing to say…I'd rather be a live mouse than a dead boss.

RALPH'S GREATEST SPEECHES

Ralph has tickets to a hit Broadway show, but before he can get out the door his mother-in-law reveals the surprise ending. Ralph flies into a rage and kicks her out of the apartment. Alice is so mad that she leaves with her mother. Now, Ralph is lonely and wants to get Alice back. Norton has an idea: record an apology and send it to Alice. Ralph is dictating his "apology" on Norton's recording machine — and building up a head of steam as he speaks.

Ralph: Hello Alice, this is me, Ralph. Alice, I'm sorry. I'm miserable without ya. Please come back to me Alice, I apologize for everything I said. I even apologize to your mother. I know she doesn't mean the things she says Alice, it's just her nature. She doesn't mean to be mean, she's just born that way. When she says things about your old boyfriends and about the furniture in the apartment, I know that she doesn't mean to get me mad, she's just naturally mean, that's all. When she spilled the beans about the end of the play I shouldn'ta got mad at that, I should've expected it from 'er. I know how she is. She's never gonna be any different Alice. She's gonna be the same old way Alice! She's a blaaaaabermouthhhh!!! A blaaaaabermouthhhh!!!

*The Racoon Lodge's annual fishing trip is coming up,
and once again the Racoons have unanimously voted
to leave their wives at home. However, when Ralph
makes a motion that the Racoons tell their wives
they're not invited, none of the Racoons will back him
up. So Ralph decides to lecture them.*

Ralph: Sure, just as I figured, you all vote that the
women are not comin' on the fishin' trip. Big men!
But what does it mean? Nothin! Because when it
comes time to face your wife you all back down and
give in, that's why! It's time to ask yourself a question:
Are the Racoons mice or men?

Racoon: Now wait a minute Kramden, how come your
wife was always on the fishing trip?

Ralph: Because I let her come, that's why. Because I let
her come, that's why! And do you know why I let 'er
come? Because I didn't wanna show you guys up,
that's why! Now look, I'm gonna say somethin' to you
men and you better listen to it because it's important.
Every time that you get into the habit of saying "yes"
to your wife, you're getting into the habit of saying
"no" to your independence. It's time to make a
decision men, are you gonna retreat into the darkness
of slavery, or are you going to advance, advance into
the sunshine of freedom?!?

Racoons: Here, here!

Ralph: This is our last chance! If we let these women take over our fishing trip we are through, all is lost! Remember, today it's the fishing trip, tomorrow it'll be the pool room!

The Kramdens have learned that a suitcase full of money that Ralph found on his bus — and has been spending all over town — is counterfeit. He's just returned from the police station and now has to face Alice.

Alice: All I know is, that if you had listened to me none of this would've happened. But no, Ralph, you never listen to anyone...but yourself.

Ralph: Are you finished? Are you finished with all the lectures, Carrie Nation? Are you finished with the, "If you only hadda done what I told you so's"? Are you finished with those?!? Well if you're finished with 'em let's get something clear, right now! So what? So what if I got in a little trouble? I was a millionaire for a couple of days. That's more than anybody else in this dump can say. For two days I had it and I went with it, too. It came easy and it went just as fast. And that's the way I'd be if I had it...easy come, easy go. If anybody found out I had it, they could have it. It's my nature to spend...'cept I never have anything to spend.

Ralph thinks he is inheriting $40 million from an old lady he used to help on and off his bus. Alice is concerned that Ralph's going to cheat Norton out of his share, which he is entitled to as a "stockholder" in Ralph Kramden, Inc.

Ralph: In a few hours I am gonna be a very rich man.
Alice: Ralph, all I'm saying is, don't count your chickens before they're hatched. And remember, Norton gets thirty-five percent of those chickens.
Ralph: Don't worry, I can take care of him.
Alice: What do you mean? Ralph, you wouldn't cheat Norton out of his share?
Ralph: Of course not, I'm not gonna cheat 'im, just gonna try to do what's best for everybody. You know how people act when they get a lotta money, they go nuts. You know how Norton is, he's the nervous type. He'd really go nuts if he got his hands on anything. First thing you know he'd quit his job in the sewer,

next thing he'd do is buy clothes, buy automobiles, yachts, start taking a tour around the world. Drinking champagne, eatin' caviar. First thing you know he wouldn't come home. Poor Trixie pleading' with 'im, "Please come home Norton." Him laughin' at her. That'd be a nice thing, wouldn't it, after all she's done for him, pleadin' for him to come home and him laughin' at 'er? Well, if you think that I'm gonna do that to such a nice girl like Trixie, you're crazy!

The Kramdens and Nortons have had a night out at an amusement park and Ralph is reminiscing about his younger days with Alice.

Ralph: You know, doing all those silly things that we did reminded me of when we really were kids, Alice. Remember that? We used to go dancin' and rollerskatin', everything. Loop the loops! Remember when it was all over at night, we used to go to the

Chinese restaurant and have some Chinese food. Had a whole dinner for sixty cents. I used to order the chop suey, you'd get the fried rice, then we'd split it. I kept askin' the guy for bread, he says, "We have no bread here, it's a Chinese restaurant." "How'm I gonna push it on the fork?" I used to con 'em, he used to bring the bread. Boy those were the days, I'm tellin' you.

Alice: Ralph, do you remember the dances we used to go to at the Sons of Italy Hall?

Ralph: Yeah, yeah, yeah! They had some good bands in that joint, too. Isham Jones, Ted Fio Rito, Little Jack Little.

Norton: Not to forget Basil Fomeen!

Ralph: Basil Fomeen!

Norton: Johnny Messler and his toy piano!

Ralph: You know something, talking like this, it teaches you one thing — acting young isn't what keeps you young, but if you got some memories, some *good memories* of when you were young, that's what keeps you young. Thinkin' about it in your old age, when you were a kid, all the things that you did. That's the whole secret of it. You know, it's a shame, I read someplace one time and the guy was right about it, too, I think it was Bernard Shaw. He says it's a shame that youth has to be wasted on young people. He's right, too.

Ralph thinks that following Norton's astrological advice has ruined his chance for a raise at the bus company.

Ralph: Do you realize what he's done to me? He cost me my raise. My raise would have been *at least* two dollars a week! You know what that adds up to during the year? A hundred dollars! And in twenty years it's two thousand dollars! Do you know what we coulda done with two thousand dollars Alice? We coulda got a home on Long Island in the suburbs. Every afternoon and morning I woulda had to commute. Do you know what happens when you're commutin'? Ya meet people! Nice people! I mighta met some guy, he woulda said to me, "Ralph, I like you. Come over to the country club and play golf," or somethin'. I woulda gone over there and played golf, woulda met all kinds of people. People come from all over the world to play golf on Long Island! Sooner or later I woulda met some guy from Texas. Played golf with 'em, he takes a likin' to me. All of a sudden, one day we're in the clubhouse and he gives me a tip on an oil well or somethin'. I invest in it, the first thing you know eighty barrel come gushin' up. Eighty barrels a day! Make enough money to buy my own oil well. How about that bum Norton! On accounta him I don't have my own oil well!

Ralph's lodge, the Racoons, is roasting one of its members, Stanley Saxon, who plans to marry Ralph's sister-in-law. All is going well until Ralph learns that Stanley has agreed to move in with his in-laws after the wedding.

Ralph: You can't do that Stanley, you'll be making the biggest mistake of your life! Take it from me, I know. When Alice and I got married, we moved in with them, you know, just for a short while till I got on my feet and got straightened out. They were six of the most miserable years I ever spent in my life! You won't be allowed to make *one* decision by yourself! And they'll keep tellin' you that you're only a guest in the house.

Stanley: Oh, I don't know Ralph, they seem like nice people.

Ralph: They seem like nice people? Sure they seem like nice people, *now* they seem like nice people. Boris Karloff seems like a nice guy when he's dancin' on the Red Skelton show, too, you know. Did y'ever see 'im in *Frankenstein*? That's the *real* Karloff, and you'll meet the *real* relatives when you move into that house.

Stanley: But it's too late now, Ralph, Agnes has already made up her mind.

Ralph: Agnes has made up her mind? Agnes has made

up her mind?!? What's the matter with you Stanley? This is the U.S.A., the twentieth century. *She* made up her mind. Who cares if *she* made up her mind? Don't forget, you are the king, because a man's home is his castle. And in that castle you're the king, you're the king of your castle!

Stanley: But Agnes was very definite about it Ralph, I don't want to argue.

Norton? Well if you don't want to argue, whaddya gettin' married for?

Ralph: Stanley, if you take my advice, tomorrow afternoon when Agnes says "I do," that is the last decision you allow her to make. From there on in, show her who wears the pants. Now, a little toast to Stanley, who is the king of his castle!

Norton: To the king!

Ralph: To the king! Ha ha ha!